DISCARD

DISCARD

DEADLY AND INCREDIBLE ANIMALS
TOP 10 Dinosaurs

Jay Dale

This edition first published in 2012 in the United States of America by Smart Apple Media. All rights reserved. No part of this book may be reproduced in any form or by any means without written permission from the publisher.

Smart Apple Media
P.O. Box 3263
Mankato, MN, 56002

First published in 2011 by
MACMILLAN EDUCATION AUSTRALIA PTY LTD
15–19 Claremont St, South Yarra, Australia 3141

Visit our web site at www.macmillan.com.au or go directly to
www.macmillanlibrary.com.au

Associated companies and representatives throughout the world.

Copyright text © Jay Dale 2011

Library of Congress Cataloging-in-Publication Data

Dale, Jay.
    Top ten dinosaurs / Jay Dale.
        p. cm. — (Deadly and incredible animals)
    Summary: "Gives general information on features of dinosaurs and what happened to them. Counts down the top ten most dangerous dinosaurs using a deadliness scale"— Provided by publisher.
    Includes index.
    ISBN 978-1-59920-409-3 (lib. bdg.)
    1. Dinosaurs--Juvenile literature. I. Title.
    QE861.5.D25 2012
    567.9—dc22
                                            2010049502

Publisher: Carmel Heron
Commissioning Editor: Niki Horin
Managing Editor: Vanessa Lanaway
Proofreader: Georgina Garner
Designer: Cristina Neri, Canary Graphic Design
Page layout: Peter Shaw, Julie Thompson and Cristina Neri
Photo researcher: Legendimages
Illustrators: Andrew Craig and Nives Porcellato (maps);
Melissa Webb (pp. 18–19, 28–9); Bookmatrix, pp. 7 (bottom), 10, 11, 17, 23, 26, 27
Production Controller: Vanessa Johnson

Manufactured in China by Macmillan Production (Asia) Ltd.
Kwun Tong, Kowloon, Hong Kong
Supplier Code: CP February 2011

Acknowledgments
The author and publisher are grateful to the following for permission to reproduce copyright material:

Front cover photograph: Illustration of Tyrannosaurus rex courtesy of John Sibbick.

Photographs courtesy of: Corbis/Frans Lanting, **8**; Dreamstime.com/S100apm, **30**; Getty/DEA Picture Library, **7** (top right), **15**; iStockphoto/Allan Tooley, **5**; NASA/JPL, **9** (both); Photolibrary/DEA Picture Library, **7** (top left), /Juniors Bildarchiv, **6**, /OSF, **12**, /Photo Researchers, **21**, /SPL/Christian Jegou Publiphoto Diffusion, **13**, /SPL/Roger Harris, **20**, **24**, /SPL/Walter Myers, **4**, /SPL/Joe Tucciarone, **3**, **14**, **16**; Shutterstock/Ralf Juergen Kraft, **22**, /Bob Orsillo, **25**. Dinosaur silhouette with 'That's incredible!' feature © Shutterstock/Vule, **10**, **12**, **14**, **16**, **18**, **20**, **22**, **24**, **26**, **28**.

While every care has been taken to trace and acknowledge copyright, the publisher tenders their apologies for any accidental infringement where copyright has proved untraceable. They would be pleased to come to a suitable arrangement with the rightful owner in each case.

CONTENTS

Deadly and Incredible Animals   4

Deadly and Incredible Dinosaurs   5

Features of Dinosaurs   6

What Happened to the Dinosaurs?   8

TOP 10 DEADLY AND INCREDIBLE DINOSAURS

Number 10: EOCARCHARIA   10

Number 9: CARCHARODONTOSAURUS   12

Number 8: SPINOSAURUS   14

Number 7: TROODON   16

Number 6: VELOCIRAPTOR   18

Number 5: DEINONYCHUS   20

Number 4: UTAHRAPTOR   22

Number 3: ALLOSAURUS   24

Number 2: GIGANOTOSAURUS   26

Number 1: TYRANNOSAURUS   28

Modern Relatives of Dinosaurs   30

Glossary   31

Index   32

GLOSSARY WORDS
When a word is printed in **bold**, you can look up its meaning in the Glossary on page 31.

DEADLY AND INCREDIBLE ANIMALS

Many animals are deadly to other animals. They are deadly to their prey and sometimes even to their **predators**. Over many thousands of years, these animals have developed incredible behaviors and features to find food, to defend themselves from predators, and to protect their young.

Deadly and Incredible Features and Behaviors

Different types of animals have different deadly features and behaviors. Deadly and incredible features include strong jaws, razor-sharp teeth, and stingers or fangs for injecting **venom** into prey. Deadly and incredible behaviors include stalking, hunting, and distracting prey before attacking and killing it.

Animals such as lions use their incredible size and strength to smash, crush, and rip apart their prey. Excellent eyesight helps many **nocturnal** animals hunt their prey under the cover of even the darkest night.

▶ Meat-eating dinosaurs, such as suchomimuses, used their powerful jaws to crush their prey.

DEADLY AND INCREDIBLE DINOSAURS

Some of the most deadly and incredible animals lived on Earth about 225 million years ago.

How Do We Know about Dinosaurs?

Dinosaurs lived on Earth for 160 million years, but died out about 65 million years ago. Scientists have used **fossils** to gather as much information as possible about dinosaurs. **Paleontologists** put this information together like the pieces of a puzzle.

Theropods

Dinosaurs can be sorted into groups according to their features. The dinosaurs featured in this book belong to the theropod group (meat-eating dinosaurs). Fossils show us that some theropods were scaly, while others had feathers.

IN THIS BOOK

In this book you will read about the top 10 deadliest dinosaurs — from number 10 (least deadly) to number 1 (most deadly). There are many different opinions on which of the dinosaurs should top this list. The dinosaurs in this book have been selected on the basis of research by paleontologists.

◀ Therapods were vicious and frightening predators that sometimes hunted plant-eating dinosaurs.

FEATURES OF DINOSAURS

Theropods used their deadly behaviors and fearsome features to kill their prey. Some theropods were huge, with massive heads and razor-sharp teeth. Other, smaller, theropods were just as deadly and used cunning and intelligence to hunt down their prey.

Teeth

Most theropods had razor-sharp teeth. They used their teeth to kill their prey with one deadly bite, usually to the neck or belly.

Jaws

Many meat-eating dinosaurs used their powerful jaws to crush their prey. Their jaws were so strong they could crush bones.

That's Incredible!

Theropods often had bits of old meat stuck in their teeth. This old, rotting meat was full of germs. If a victim was bitten by a dinosaur but escaped, sometimes it would die later from the germs in the bite wound.

▶ Theropods, such as tyrannosauruses, used their sharp teeth to rip through flesh.

Claws

Many dinosaurs had large hooked claws on their front hands and **hind** feet. They used their claws to rip apart their prey.

▶ Theropods could smell their prey from long distances away.

▲ Theropods such as dromiceiomimuses had sharp claws for holding or slashing their prey.

Eyesight and Smell

Dinosaurs such as troodons, had large eyes with **binocular vision**. Dinosaurs also had a good sense of smell.

Size

Large theropods used their size to knock their prey to the ground. They had enormous heads, strong necks, thick bodies, and powerful legs.

▶ Some theropods used their enormous weight and size to stun their prey, sometimes killing them instantly.

WHAT HAPPENED TO THE DINOSAURS?

Around 65 million years ago, there were large changes to Earth, which caused dinosaurs to become **extinct**.

Volcanic Activity

Scientists believe that there was a lot of volcanic activity around the time dinosaurs died out. Their research shows that there were many volcanic explosions during the last part of the Cretaceous period, around 99.5 to 65.5 million years ago. These explosions released gases and smoke into the atmosphere.

Volcanic ash would have blocked out sunlight. This would have caused plants to stop growing, which would have affected the **food chain**. Plant-eating dinosaurs would have died out first, then the theropods would have died, because there was no prey to eat.

▼ When a volcano explodes, hot lava flows over Earth's surface, killing everything in its path.

A Big Impact

Many scientists believe that a large **asteroid** crashed into Earth about 65 million years ago. The impact of this asteroid would have caused many volcanic explosions, landslides, and earthquakes around the world. There could have been enormous waves, called tsunamis, destroying habitats.

Scientists are not certain if the dinosaurs were living a healthy existence before the asteroid impact. It is possible that dinosaurs had started to die out before the impact, due to volcanic activity. The impact may have brought about the end of a slow **extinction**, or it could have caused a sudden extinction of all dinosaurs. We may never know.

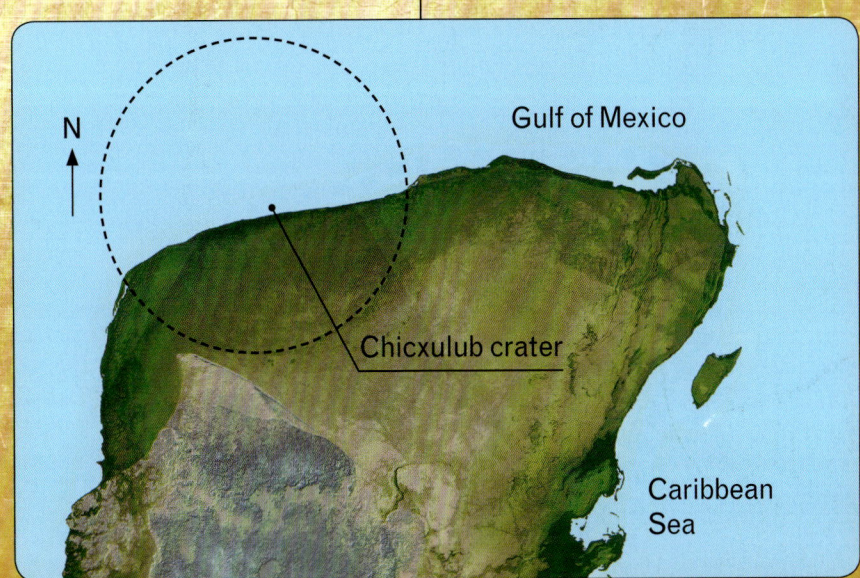

▶ Scientists believe the massive Chicxulub crater in Mexico was formed when a huge asteroid hit Earth. The crater is more than 112 miles (180 km) wide.

NUMBER 10

EOCARCHARIA

(say *EE-oh-car-CAR-ee-ah*) Greek for "dawn shark"

- band of bone for ramming
- razor-sharp teeth
- claws
- massive hind legs

The eocarcharia lived on land, but it is named for its shark-like teeth and powerful jaws.

That's Incredible! The eocarcharia's full name, *Eocarcharia dinops*, means "fierce-eyed dawn shark." This refers to the menacing look of the band of bone above its eyes.

◀ An eocarcharia had a huge head with a thick band of bone above its eyes.

FACT FILE

Deadly features: band of bone, sharp teeth, claws
Predators: none
Size: length 26 to 40 feet (8–12 m); weight 990 pounds (450 kg)
Lifespan: unknown
When it lived: 110 million years ago
Habitat: woodlands

Distribution: ■ Northern Africa

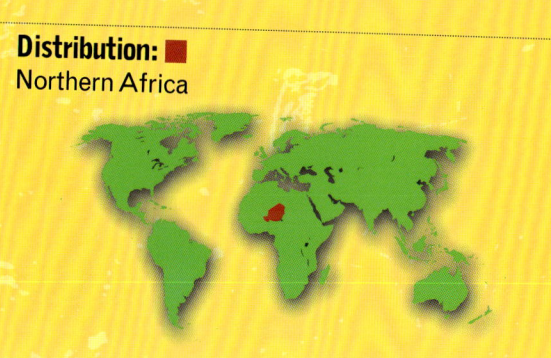

Head-butting Behavior

This large and clumsy dinosaur used its enormous head to ram its prey and **rivals**. The eocarcharia used its sharp claws and massive hind legs to pin down its prey, while its teeth cut up the body parts.

Top Predator

It is believed that there were three other types of large meat-eating predators living in the same area as eocarcharia. These were the kryptops, suchomimus, and sarcosuchus. The kryptops fed on animals that were already dead, and the suchomimus and sarcosuchus mostly ate fish. The eocarcharia hunted living dinosaurs. It probably feasted on the plant-eating dinosaur, the nigersaurus.

What's for Dinner?

Eocarcharias ate plant-eating dinosaurs, such as nigersauruses.

▼ The eocarcharia was the most dangerous meat-eating dinosaur in northern Africa about 110 million years ago.

NUMBER 9
CARCHARODONTOSAURUS

(say *kar-KAR-o-don-toe-sor-us*) Greek for "jagged teeth lizard"

The carcharodontosaurus had a head the size of a human: about 5.5 feet (1.68 m)! Its massive jaws and long **serrated** teeth were incredibly destructive to its prey.

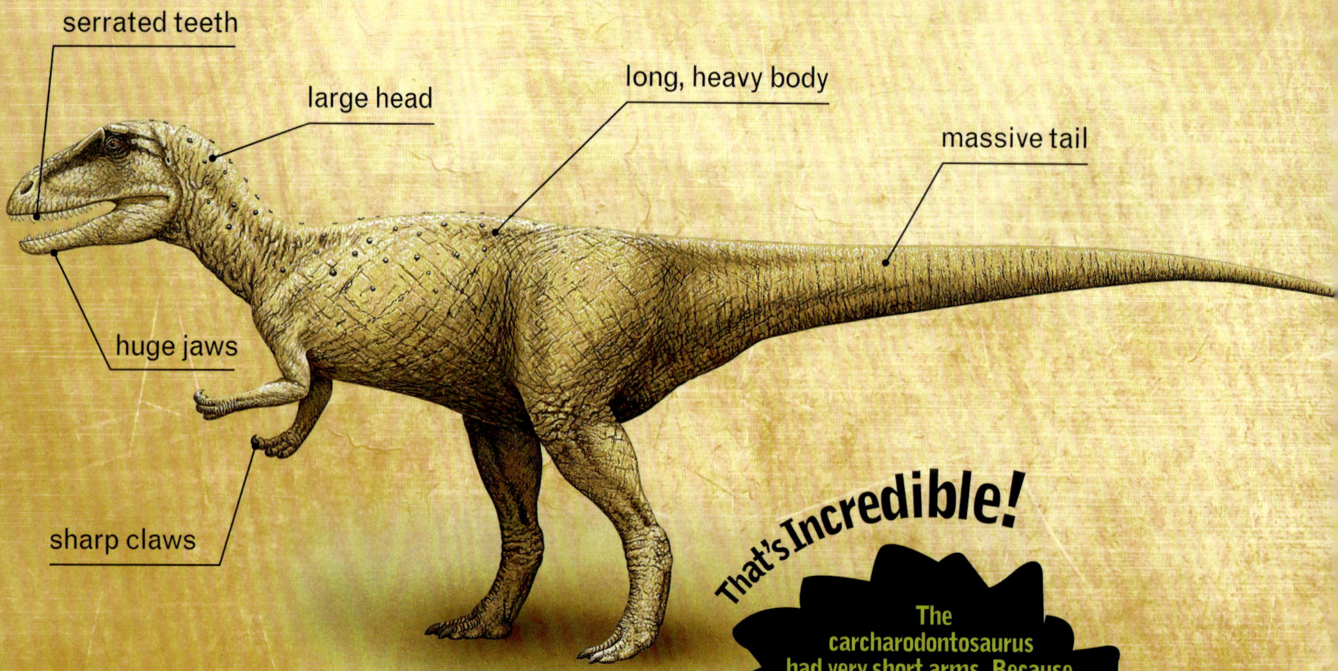

- serrated teeth
- large head
- long, heavy body
- massive tail
- huge jaws
- sharp claws

▲ A carcharodontosaurus had a huge body and very heavy bones.

That's Incredible!
The carcharodontosaurus had very short arms. Because of this, scientists believe it did not run at full speed. Its arms were not big enough to protect it if it fell while running at a fast pace.

FACT FILE

Deadly features: serrated teeth, sharp claws, powerful jaws
Predators: unknown
Size: length 44 feet (13.5 m)
Lifespan: unknown
When it lived: 98 to 93 million years ago
Habitat: woodlands, desert

Distribution: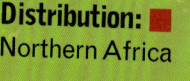
Northern Africa

Fierce Predator

The carcharodontosaurus was a fierce predator. Its huge, powerful jaws could devour mouthfuls of flesh the size of a human! It was able to kill much larger plant-eating dinosaurs, such as **sauropods**. Like many of the meat-eating dinosaurs of its time it was also a scavenger that ate rotting meat or unfinished prey left by other theropods. Scientists believe it may have hunted in packs, or groups.

Flesh-tearing Claws

The carcharodontosaurus had three-fingered hands with sharp claws that would rip its prey to shreds. Its serrated teeth were 6 inches (15 cm) long and it used them to tear the flesh.

What's for Dinner?
Carcharodontosauruses ate a range of small to large dinosaurs, including sauropods.

▼ For a carcharodontosaurus, small plant-eating dinosaurs were a quick, tasty snack.

NUMBER 8

SPINOSAURUS

(say *SPINE-oh-SOR-us*) Greek for "spine lizard"

The spinosaurus was one of the largest meat-eating dinosaurs. It had long jaws and a large sail along its back. It probably used its jaws to catch fish. It may have used the sail to soak up the warmth of the sun.

long jaws

sail

sharp teeth

◀ The spinosaurus was one of the biggest meat-eating dinosaurs.

hook-like claws

That's Incredible!

The first spinosaurus remains were discovered in Egypt in 1911, but they were destroyed in 1944 during World War II. A lot of what is known about spinosauruses comes from skull material found in Morocco and Algeria in later years.

FACT FILE

Deadly features: long arms with three claws, long jaws filled with sharp teeth
Predators: none
Size: length 50 to 60 feet (16–18 m); height 15 to 20 feet (4.8–6 m); weight 7 to 9 tons (7–9 t)
Lifespan: unknown
When it lived: 95 to 70 million years ago
Habitat: mangrove forests, tidal flats

Distribution: Northern Africa

Spiny Sail

The spinosaurus' sail was made up of long spines. These spines were up to 5.6 feet (1.7 m) long. Some scientists believe this sail was used to attract a mate, but others believe it was used to warm up and cool down its body. Some even say it was used to scare away rivals.

A Mysterious Dinosaur

Not much is known about the spinosaurus. Some scientists believe it was probably an opportunistic hunter, eating any animals that came along. However, some scientists believe it was a vicious hunter similar to the tyrannosaurus. Others say it was a gentle fish-eating dinosaur. Unless new **evidence** is found, the spinosaurus will remain a mystery.

What's for Dinner?
Some scientists think that fish was only a part of the diet of spinosauruses.

▶ Spinosaurus may have been a vicious dinosaur, hunting many different kinds of prey.

NUMBER 7

TROODON

(say *TROH-o-don*) Greek for "wounding tooth"

Although the troodon was only the size of an adult human, it was a fearsome hunter. Its lightweight body and long legs made it an incredibly fast runner, which would have been useful when chasing its prey.

large eyes

▼ The troodon's large eyes suggest it may have been a nocturnal hunter.

light body

tail to help with balance

claws

That's Incredible!

The troodon had long arms that folded back just like a bird's wings. Its forearms were more flexible than other theropods with shorter arms.

FACT FILE

Deadly features: excellent eyesight and hearing, swift movement, sharp claws and teeth
Predators: unknown
Size: length 6.5 feet (2 m); weight 133 pounds (60 kg)
Lifespan: unknown
When it lived: 75 to 65 million years ago
Habitat: plains

Distribution: ◼
Mongolia and North America

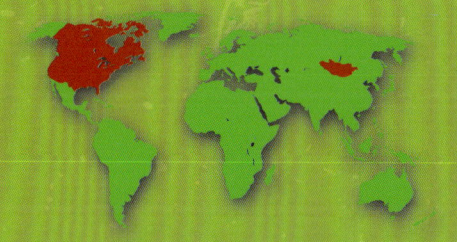

Fast and Ferocious Hunter

The troodon's excellent eyesight and hearing, sharp claws, razor-sharp teeth, and swift movement made it a deadly predator. Although it did not have the size and the weight of the larger dinosaurs, its speed and its ability to move quickly and easily gave it an advantage.

What's for Dinner?

Troodons ate smaller animals, such as lizards and snakes, some plants, and dinosaur hatchlings.

Smartest Dinosaur?

When scientists compare the troodon's brain size to its body weight it seems likely that it was very intelligent for a dinosaur. Because of its big brain, scientists believe the troodon may have been as smart as modern-day opossums.

▶ Scientists believe the troodon probably ate anything it could get its very sharp teeth into.

NUMBER 6

VELOCIRAPTOR

(say *ve-LOSS-i-RAP-tor*) Greek for "speedy thief"

The velociraptor was small but deadly. Although it weighed less than a three-year-old child, the velociraptor aggressively hunted heavy plant-eating dinosaurs. It used its sharp, curved claws to slice through the flesh of its prey.

- excellent eyesight
- serrated teeth
- long tail to help with balance
- light body
- feathers
- sharp claws
- long legs

◀ The velociraptor was an unusual-looking dinosaur. Most theropods were covered in scales, but fossils indicate the velociraptor was covered in feathers.

That's Incredible!

In 1971 fossils of a velociraptor and a protoceratops, a plant-eating dinosaur, were found in the Gobi Desert, in Mongolia. Both dinosaurs had died locked in battle, with the velociraptor clutching the protoceratop's snout while kicking it in the neck.

FACT FILE

Deadly features: excellent eyesight, swift movement, sharp teeth and claws
Predators: unknown
Size: length 6 feet (1.8 m); weight 33 pounds (15 kg)
Lifespan: unknown
When it lived: 85 to 80 million years ago
Habitat: desert

Distribution: ■
Russia, China, and Mongolia

Chasing Prey

The velociraptor was built for chasing prey. Its small, light body and long legs meant it could move quickly and easily and run very fast. Scientists believe that it may have run as fast as 37 miles (60 km) an hour when hunting. At these speeds, it would have quickly outrun a plant-eating dinosaur. The velociraptor's long, bony tail helped it balance when changing direction during a high-speed chase.

What's for Dinner?
Velociraptors ate plant-eating dinosaurs such as protoceratops, lizards, small mammals, and dinosaur eggs.

Killer Claws

The velociraptor attacked its prey using its curved claws. It had four sets of claws, but it was the largest ones that were the most dangerous. The velociraptor jumped onto its prey and used the large claws at the end of its feet to viciously stab into the flesh.

▼ The velociraptor used its deadly claws to attack its prey and its razor-sharp teeth to bite off chunks of flesh.

NUMBER 5
DEINONYCHUS
(say *die-NON-ee-kuss*) Greek for "terrible claw"

The deinonychus was built to kill. It was such a good hunter it could take down dinosaurs many times its own size.

That's Incredible!
In 2010, scientists studied puncture marks in a bone made by the teeth of a deinonychus. From this study they determined that the bite force of a deinonychus was equal to the bite force of a large alligator!

large eyes

serrated teeth

▶ A deinonychus had around 60 blade-like teeth, which it used to slice its prey to pieces.

hooked claw

sharp claws

FACT FILE

Deadly features: sharp teeth and claws, speed
Predators: unknown
Size: length 11.8 feet (3.6 m); weight 155 pounds (70 kg)
Lifespan: unknown
When it lived: 115 to 108 million years ago
Habitat: forests

Distribution:
North America

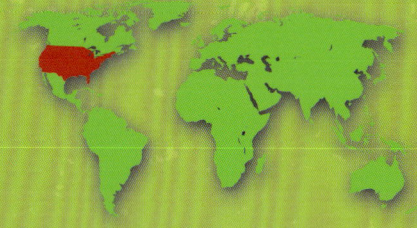

Killer Claws

The deinonychus had enormous curved claws on its second toe. Most likely these claws were held up while it walked on its third and fourth toes. Scientists think the claws were used either to cut and slash prey or to stab and puncture prey.

Hunting in Packs

It is believed this quick and clever predator may have hunted in groups. Some paleontologists believe deinonychuses may have attacked larger dinosaurs by leaping on the backs of other deinonychuses in packs. Modern-day wolves do the same thing when they attack a large moose.

What's for Dinner?
Deinonychuses ate plant-eating dinosaurs such as the ornithopod.

▼ A pack of deinonychuses could surround and attack large plant-eating dinosaurs.

NUMBER 4

UTAHRAPTOR

(say YOO-tah-RAP-tor) Greek for "Utah thief"

The utahraptor was probably the largest raptor (bird-like dinosaur) that ever lived. Scientists believe it had a large brain and was the most intelligent of the dinosaurs.

bony tail

teeth

sharp eyesight

That's Incredible!
The utahraptor's long tail would have helped it keep its balance while kicking its prey. A kick with those powerful legs and huge claws would have caused incredible injury or death to its prey.

▶ The utahraptor used its stiff bony tail for balance when running, leaping, or kicking.

hooked claws

FACT FILE

Deadly features: sharp claws, including a hooked claw on each foot, sharp teeth
Predators: unknown
Size: length 16 to 23 feet (5 to 7 m); weight 1,100 pounds (500 kg)
Lifespan: unknown
When it lived: 112 to 100 million years ago
Habitat: plains

Distribution: North America

Speedy Hunter

The utahraptor was a finely built, swift dinosaur. Many believe it was one of the fastest-moving dinosaurs. The utahraptor may have hunted in packs, killing and eating even large dinosaurs such as sauropods and **ankylosaurids**.

What's for Dinner?
Utahraptors ate other dinosaurs, such as sauropods and ankylosaurids.

Crushing Jaws and Slashing Claws

The utahraptor had a large head and powerful jaws that it used to crush prey. It had two extended "hands" with long claws. Like the deinonychus, it had a massive, hooked claw on one of its three toes. This claw was up to 1 foot (30 cm) long and was used to slash and rip apart prey.

▼ A pack of utahraptors would have used their speed to outrun large prey, such as a plant-eating dinosaur.

NUMBER 3

ALLOSAURUS

(say *AL-oh-SOR-us*) Greek for "different lizard"

The allosaurus was a deadly and vicious predator. It most likely stalked and ate large plant-eating dinosaurs up to three times its own size!

- excellent eyesight
- powerful neck for supporting a heavy head
- large, powerful jaws
- ▼ The allosaurus had excellent vision and a powerful sense of smell, enabling it to seek out its prey.
- short front limbs for holding down prey
- long, serrated teeth up to 1 inch (2 cm) long
- curved, sharp front claws up to 6 inches (15 cm) long

That's Incredible!

Remains of an allosaurus skull show horns just in front and above the eye sockets. These may have had been used as a sunshade, to make allosaurus look scary, or as a weapon to fight other dinosaurs.

FACT FILE

Deadly features: sharp front claws, powerful neck, long sharp teeth, excellent eyesight and smell
Predators: none
Size: length 36 to 39 feet (11–12 m); weight up to 2 tons (2 t)
Lifespan: unknown
When it lived: 154 to 140 million years ago
Habitat: plains
Distribution: North America, Portugal, central Africa

Slow But Sneaky

The allosaurus was one of the largest predators that ever lived. It roamed Earth on two powerful legs. Although it had strong back legs, it was probably a slow and heavy mover, because it was so large. Most scientists believe it was a sneaky hunter rather than a speedy hunter.

Hunting in Groups

Scientists believe allosauruses hunted in groups to **ambush** their prey. They were clever dinosaurs that stalked their prey together, just like lions do today.

What's for Dinner?

Allosauruses ate any animal they could kill, particularly **ornithischians** and smaller sauropods, such as the apatosaurus.

▲ The allosaurus used its razor-sharp teeth to rip its prey to pieces.

NUMBER 2 — GIGANOTOSAURUS

(say *JYE-ga-NO-toe-SOR-us*) Greek for "giant southern lizard"

The giganotosaurus was one of the largest creatures that ever lived on land. It was longer than a bus and it could have eaten a human in just one bite.

That's Incredible!
Based on the shape of its skull, scientists believe the giganotosaurus had a small brain and was not very intelligent. Its brain may have been the shape of a banana!

- large head
- sharp teeth
- long claws
- three-fingered hands

▶ The giganotosaurus had three-fingered hands with long, sharp claws, which were used to hold its prey and tear off flesh.

FACT FILE

Deadly features: long claws, large size, large head, sharp teeth
Predators: unknown
Size: length 46 feet (14 m); weight 8 tons (8 t)
Lifespan: unknown
When it lived: 112 to 90 million years ago
Habitat: swamps

Distribution: Argentina, in South America

Large Theropod

The giganotosaurus lived on Earth about the same time as spinosauruses but before tyrannosauruses. Although bigger than a tyrannosaurus, the giganotosaurus was probably not as powerful. It had a larger skull but its brain was smaller, its jaws less powerful, and its teeth shorter and narrower. The giganotosaurus was not quite as big as a spinosaurus.

Pack Hunters?

The fossil remains of a giganotosaurus were found close to the remains of another large dinosaur, a plant-eater called argentinosaurus. Scientists believe it would have taken many giganotosauruses to knock down one large argentinosaurus. This makes scientists think that the giganotosaurus was a pack hunter.

What's for Dinner?
Giganotosauruses ate all animals, including argentinosauruses.

▶ A giganotosaurus's short, sharp, arrow-tipped teeth suggest they were used to slice flesh rather than crunch through bone.

27

NUMBER 1

TYRANNOSAURUS

(say tye-RAN-uh-SOR-us) Greek for "tyrant lizard"

The tyrannosaurus was one of the deadliest predators ever to live on Earth. Its powerful bite could crack through the hard armor of an ankylosaurid.

- excellent eyesight
- long, stiff tail for balance
- sharp teeth
- powerful jaws
- claw-like fingers

▶ The tyrannosaurus had a stiff, pointed tail which helped it to balance and make quick turns when chasing prey.

That's Incredible! If a tyrannosaurus broke some teeth, new ones would grow back to replace the broken ones.

FACT FILE

Deadly features: sharp teeth, long tail, powerful jaws, excellent eyesight
Predators: unknown
Size: length 40 feet (12.4 m); height 15 to 20 feet (4.6–6 m); weight 6.5 tons (6.5 t)
Lifespan: about 30 years
When it lived: 67 to 66 million years ago
Habitat: semitropical open forests, coastal forested swamps

Distribution: North America

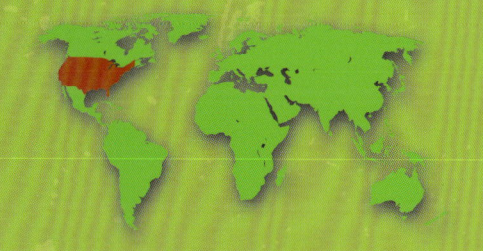

Bone-crushing Bite

A tyrannosaurus' bite was as powerful as a modern-day alligator's. It is estimated that it could eat 500 pounds (230 kg) of meat and bones in just one bite! Its jaws were up to 4 feet (1.2 m) long and 20 to 24 inches (50–60 cm) thick, and its teeth grew up to 9 inches (23 cm) long.

Claw-like Fingers

A tyrannosaurus' forearms were short and stumpy with two claw-like fingers each. Scientists believe these were used to help the tyrannosaurus stand up after lying down. Some believe they were used to hold down prey as the dinosaur tore apart the prey with its sharp teeth.

What's for Dinner?
Tyrannosauruses ate all other dinosaurs, dead or alive!

◀ With powerful legs, a huge body, strong jaws, and razor-sharp teeth, the tyrannosaurus was a deadly predator.

MODERN RELATIVES OF DINOSAURS

Today's reptiles and birds have physical features that are similar to those of meat-eating dinosaurs.

Reptiles

Reptiles are a large group of animals with scaly skin and young that hatch from eggs. Many scientists believe that meat-eating and plant-eating dinosaurs were reptiles because they had these reptilian features. Today, dinosaurs are an extinct reptile group. Some reptiles, such as crocodiles, existed before, during, and after the dinosaurs.

Birds

Nearly all paleontologists agree that birds are related to theropods. The earliest birds look very much like smaller meat-eating dinosaurs, such as troodons. Most meat-eating dinosaurs walked upright just like birds do, and had similar skulls and claws. Some scientists believe birds are "living dinosaurs."

◀ Crocodiles are reptiles that live on Earth today. They are closely related to the crocodiles that lived in dinosaur times.

GLOSSARY

Ambush Make a surprise attack on

Ankylosaurids A type of plant-eating dinosaur

Asteroid Large rock-like object from space

Binocular vision Using two eyes together

Evidence Something that proves that a belief is true

Extinct Wiped out, or no longer alive anywhere on Earth

Extinction Becoming extinct – wiped out and no longer alive anywhere on Earth

Food chain A linked system of animals, plants, and other living things in which each member is eaten in turn by another member

Fossils Remains of a living thing from long ago that have been embedded and preserved in rocks for millions of years

Habitat The environment where animals and plants live

Hind At the back

Nocturnal Active (usually hunting) at night

Ornithiscians Dinosaurs whose hips point backward, also known as bird-hipped dinosaurs

Paleontologists Scientists who study fossils

Predators Meat-eating animals that hunt, kill, and eat other animals

Rivals Enemies or other predators that may fight for the same prey

Sauropods Huge, long-necked, four-legged, plant-eating dinosaurs

Serrated Jagged, like the blade of a saw

Venom A poisonous or harmful substance produced by an animal, which is injected by bite or sting

INDEX

A
alligators 20, 29
allosaurus 24–5
ambush 25
ankylosaurids 23, 28
apatosaurus 25
argentinosaurus 27
asteroid 9

B
birds 16, 22, 30
binocular vision 7
brain 17, 22, 26, 27

C
carcharodontosaurus 12–13
Chicxulub crater 9
claws 7, 10, 11, 12, 13, 14, 15, 16, 17, 18, 19, 20, 21, 22, 23, 24, 25, 26, 27, 28, 29, 30
crocodiles 30

D
deinonychus 20–21
dromiceiomimus 7

E
eocarcharia 10–11
extinction 8–9
eyesight 4, 7, 17, 18, 19, 22, 24, 25, 28, 29

F
feathers 5, 18
fossils 5, 18, 27

G
giganotosaurus 19, 26–7

H
habitat 9, 11, 13, 15, 17, 19, 21, 23, 25, 27, 29

J
jaws 4, 6, 10, 12, 13, 14, 15, 23, 24, 27, 28, 29

K
kryptops 11

N
nigersaurus 11
nocturnal animals 4, 16

O
opportunistic hunter 15
ornithischian 25
ornithopod 21

P
paleontologists 5, 21, 30
plant-eating dinosaurs 5, 8, 11, 13, 18, 19, 21, 23, 24
predators 4, 5, 11, 13, 15, 17, 19, 21, 23, 24, 25, 27, 28, 29
protoceratops 18, 19

R
raptor 22
reptiles 30

S
sarcosuchus 11
sauropods 13, 23, 25
scavenger 13
sense of smell 7, 24, 25
snout 18
spinosaurus 14–15, 27
suchomimus 4, 11

T
tail 12, 16, 18, 19, 22, 28, 29
teeth 4, 6, 10, 11, 12, 13, 14, 15, 17, 18, 19, 20, 21, 22, 23, 24, 25, 26, 27, 28, 29, 30
theropods 5, 6, 7, 8, 13, 16, 18, 27, 30
troodon 16–17, 30
tyrannosaurus 6, 15, 27, 28–9

U
utahraptor 22–3

V
velociraptor 18–19
volcanoes 8, 9